DISCARD

HOW MUSCLES WORK

Sue Heavenrich

THE HUMAN MACHINE

rourkeeducationalmedia.com

Before & After Reading Activities

Before Reading:

Building Academic Vocabulary and Background Knowledge

Before reading a book, it is important to tap into what your child or students already know about the topic. This will help them develop their vocabulary, increase their reading comprehension, and make connections across the curriculum.

1. Look at the cover of the book. What will this book be about?
2. What do you already know about the topic?
3. Let's study the Table of Contents. What will you learn about in the book's chapters?
4. What would you like to learn about this topic? Do you think you might learn about it from this book? Why or why not?
5. Use a reading journal to write about your knowledge of this topic. Record what you already know about the topic and what you hope to learn about the topic.
6. Read the book.
7. In your reading journal, record what you learned about the topic and your response to the book.
8. After reading the book complete the activities below.

Content Area Vocabulary

Read the list. What do these words mean?

contracts
filaments
involuntary
lever
ligament
myofibrils
nutrients
striated
tissue
voluntary

After Reading:

Comprehension and Extension Activity

After reading the book, work on the following questions with your child or students in order to check their level of reading comprehension and content mastery.

1. What happens when a nerve impulse triggers a skeletal muscle contraction? (Summarize)
2. Why can't muscles push? (Infer)
3. Where can you find levers in your body? (Asking Questions)
4. How do your choices about food and physical activity affect your muscles? (Text to Self Connection)
5. How does using smartphones and other digital devices affect your muscles? (Asking Questions)

Extension Activity

Get a friend and a piece of very large paper for each of you (something bigger than you, such as butcher paper or sheets of paper taped together). You also need markers or crayons. Lie on your back on the paper and have your friend trace the outline of your body. Draw the major muscles inside your outline and label them.

TABLE OF CONTENTS

Get Moving	4
Meet the Muscles	6
Looking Closer at Skeletal Muscles	12
Muscles Move Us	18
Taking Care of Your Muscles	22
Glossary	30
Index	31
Show What You Know	31
Further Reading	31
About the Author	32

GET MOVING

You've got more than 600 muscles. They give your body shape. Without them, you'd just be a sack of skin and bones.

Muscles help you stand up and stay balanced. They move blood through your body. They move food through your digestive system.

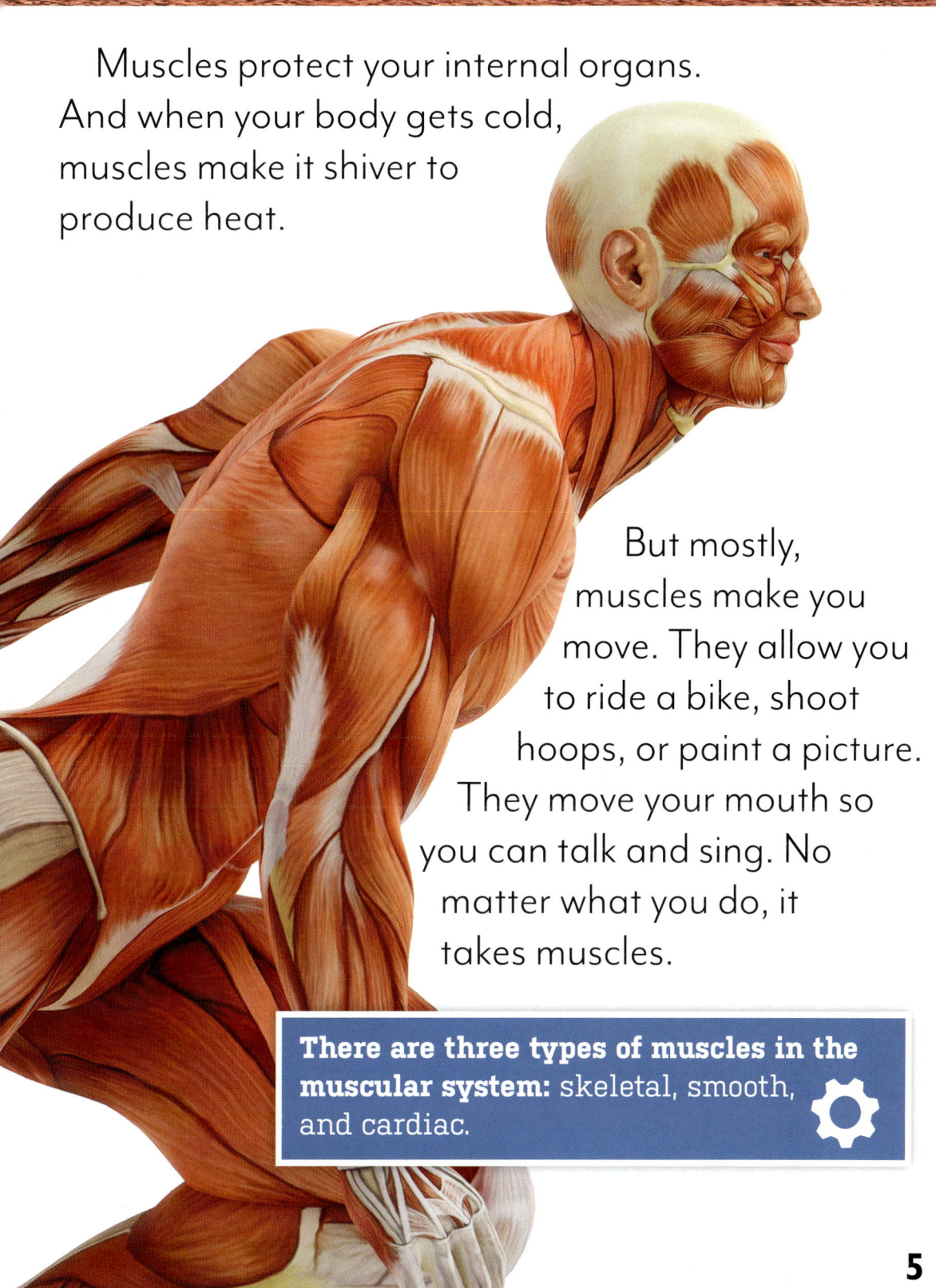

Muscles protect your internal organs. And when your body gets cold, muscles make it shiver to produce heat.

But mostly, muscles make you move. They allow you to ride a bike, shoot hoops, or paint a picture. They move your mouth so you can talk and sing. No matter what you do, it takes muscles.

There are three types of muscles in the muscular system: skeletal, smooth, and cardiac.

MEET THE MUSCLES

When most people talk about muscles, they are thinking of skeletal muscles. Those are the muscles that move you. Skeletal muscles are **voluntary** because you control what they do.

Skeletal muscles come in all sizes and shapes. Your biceps is spindle-shaped, thick in the middle and narrowed on each end. The pectoralis muscles in your chest look like fans. And the muscles around your lips and eyelids form circles. If you look at skeletal muscles under a microscope, you'll see they are **striated**. They have light and dark bands that look like stripes.

stapedius muscle

The shortest muscle is the stapedius in the inner ear. It is 1/20th of an inch (1.27 millimeter) long. The biggest muscle is the gluteus maximus. It's the one you sit on. The fastest muscle closes the eyelid. It **contracts** in less than 1/100th of a second.

6

TYPES OF MUSCLES

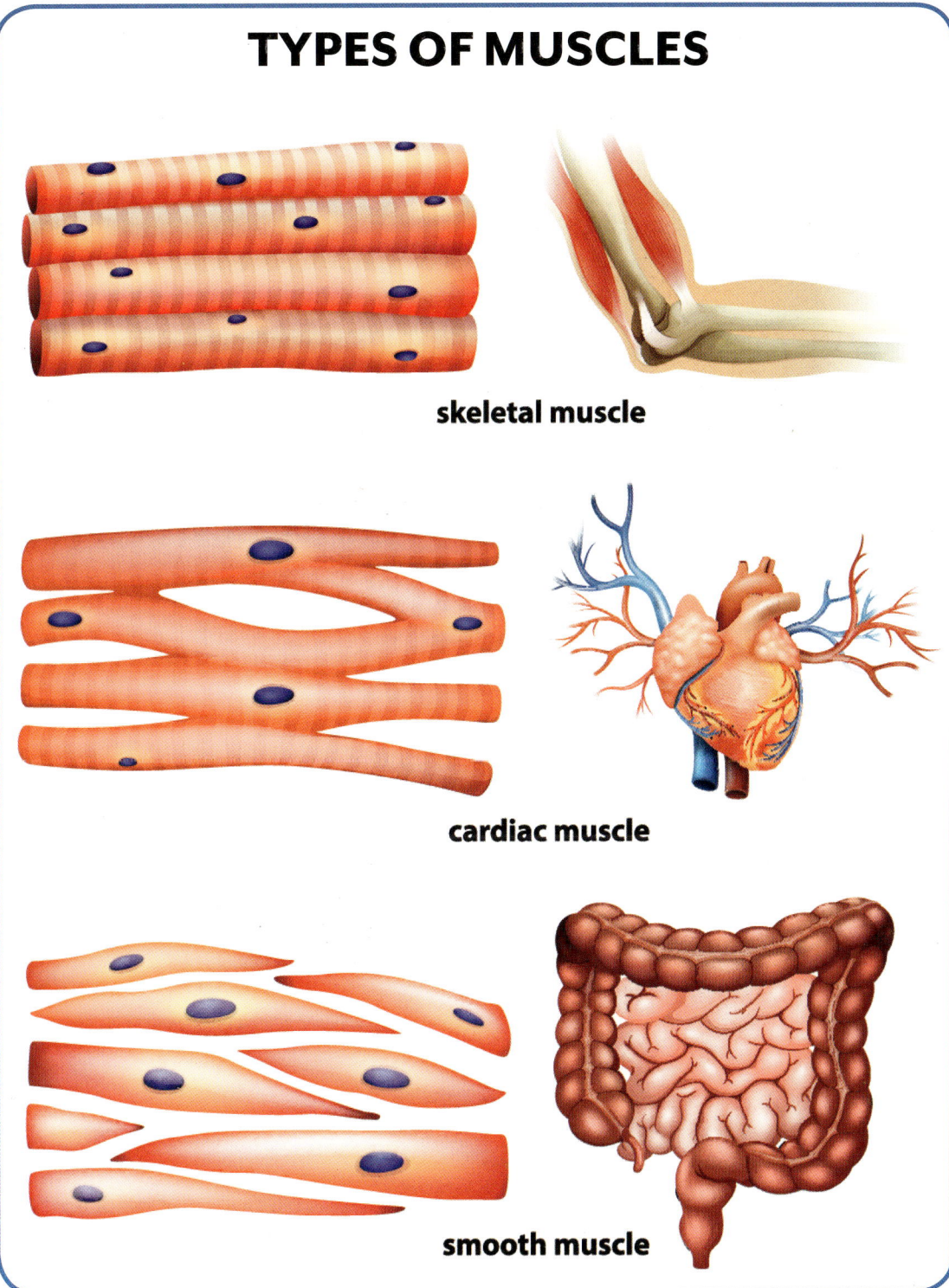

skeletal muscle

cardiac muscle

smooth muscle

Skeletal muscles are attached to bones by connective **tissue** called tendons. The tendon that attaches your calf muscle to your heel is thick and rope-like. You can feel it at the back of your ankle. Small tendons attach muscles to your eyeballs. They allow you to roll your eyes.

muscles

Achilles tendon

8

Smooth muscles make up the walls of your stomach, intestines, and other organs. These muscles form flat sheets and layers. The smooth muscle in the walls of blood vessels constricts or dilates the vessels. That determines your blood pressure.

You can't control smooth muscles. They are **involuntary**. When you swallow food, the muscles around the esophagus contract and push food to the stomach. Smooth muscles in your digestive system keep working even when you sleep.

In 1962, astronaut John Glenn ate applesauce while orbiting Earth. He showed that you don't need gravity to swallow food. That means you can swallow even when you are upside down.

Cardiac muscle makes up your heart. It's striated, like skeletal muscles. But it's involuntary. The heart beats close to 100,000 times a day with no instructions from you. In one minute, the heart pumps five quarts (4.73 liters) of blood.

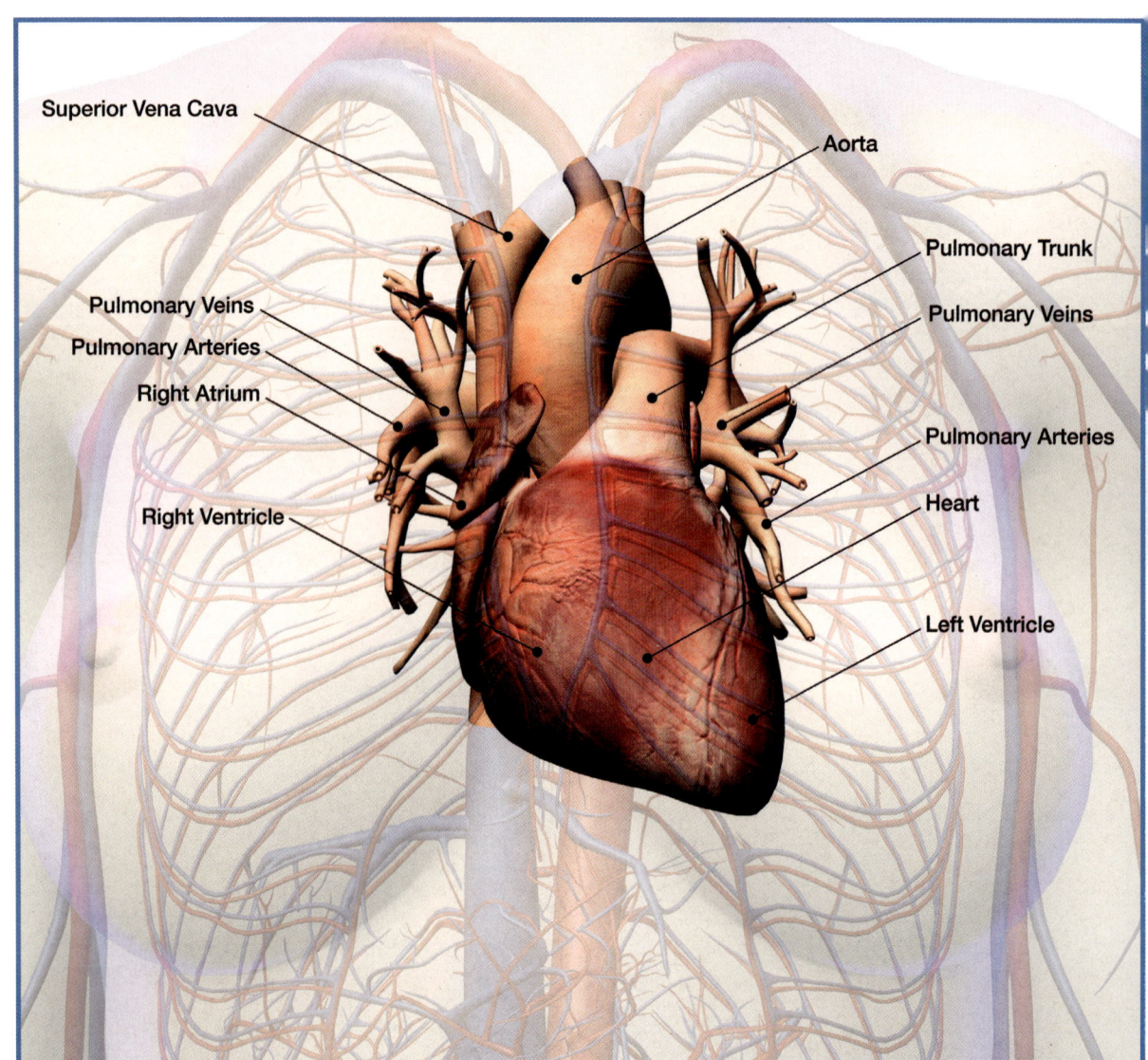

myocardium under electron microscope

This is a colored image of cardiac muscle fibers produced by a scanning electron microscope (SEM). The microscope is so powerful it allows scientists to magnify muscle tissue—and other things—more than 300,000 times. Because of the way they work, SEMs provide a nearly three-dimensional image.

Think you can work as hard as your heart? Get two buckets or dishpans. Fill one with five quarts (4.73 liters) of water. Use a 1/4 cup (60 milliliter) measure as a scoop. Set a timer for one minute and scoop water from the full pan into the empty pan. Can you move all the water before the timer buzzes?

LOOKING CLOSER AT SKELETAL MUSCLES

It's hard to see your own muscles, but if you eat chicken, peel the skin off a wing before it's cooked. See the connective tissue covering the muscles?

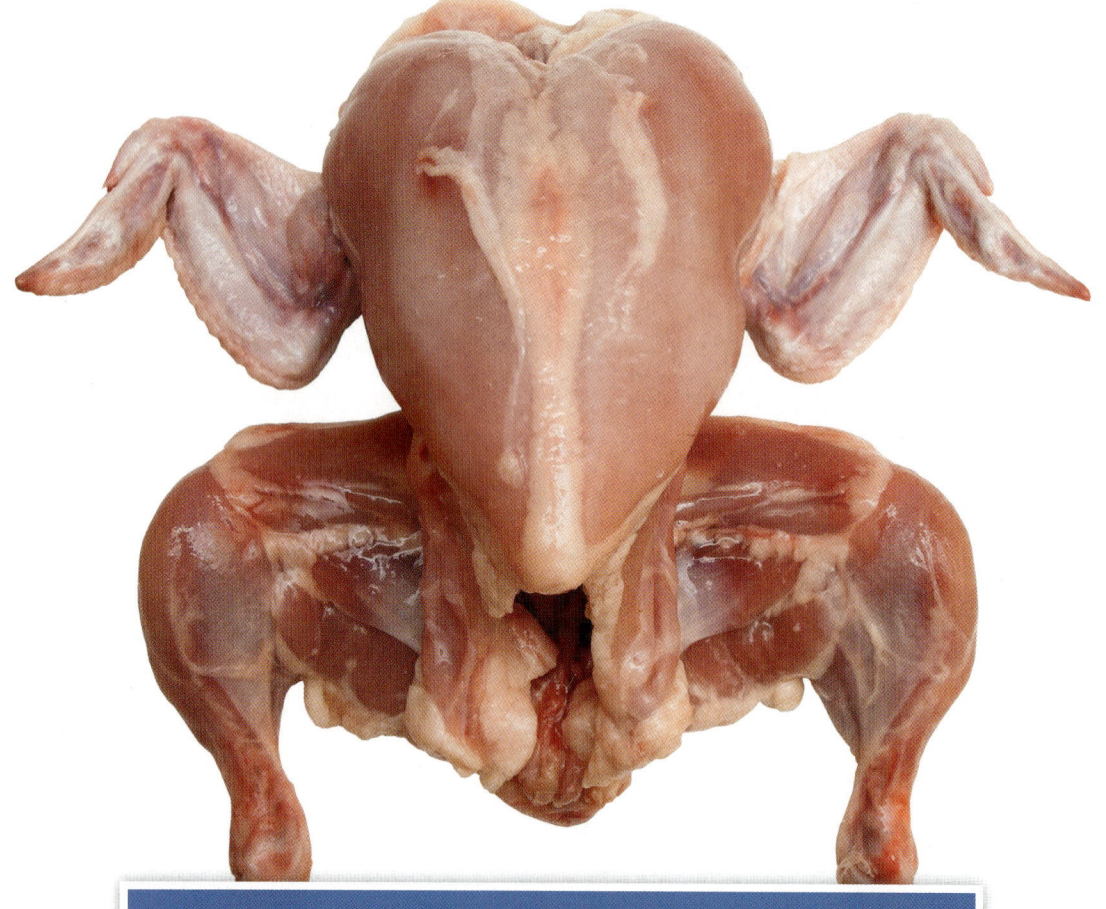

Wear rubber gloves when handling raw meat. Make sure to wash your hands with soap and water afterward.

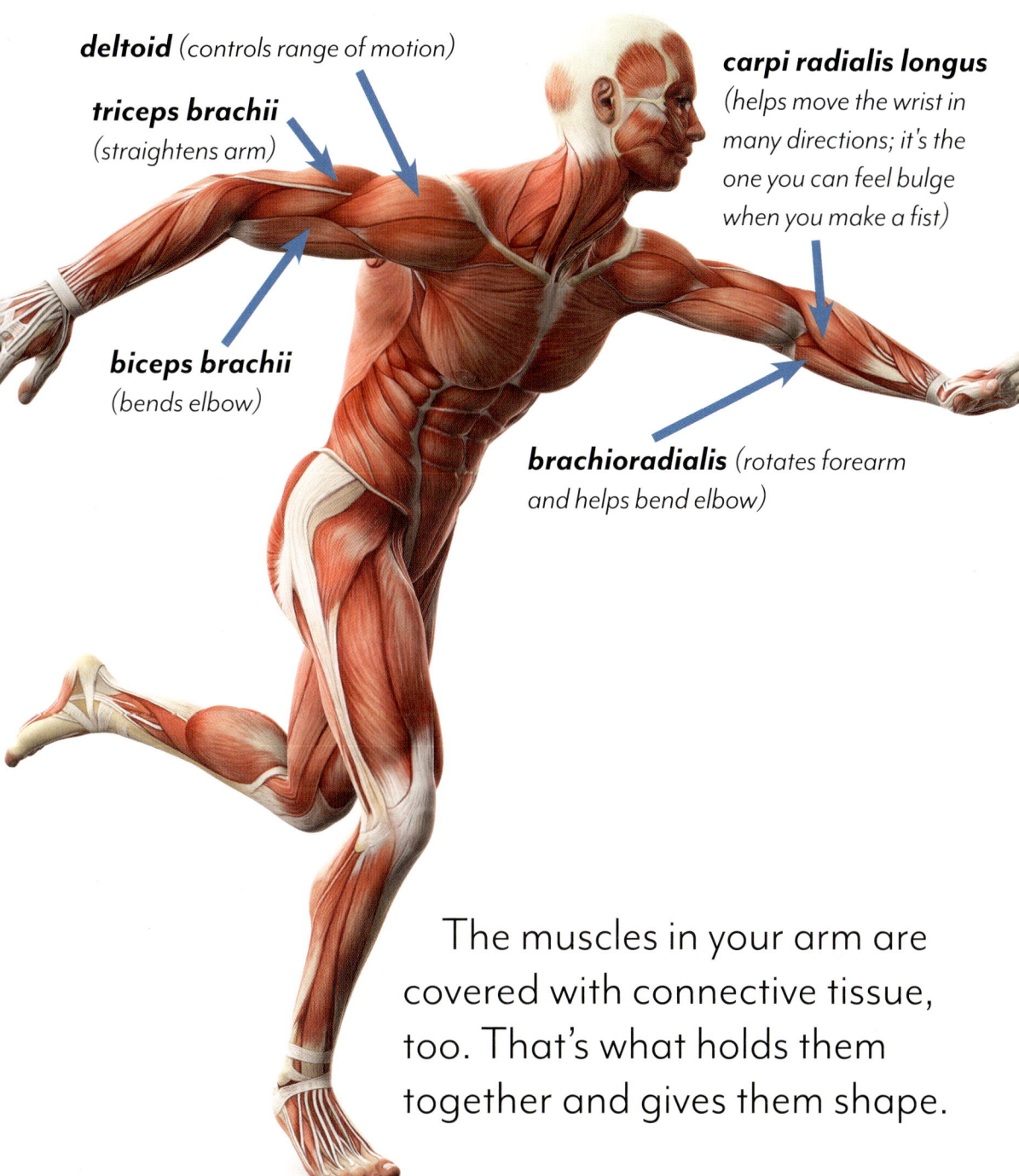

deltoid (controls range of motion)

triceps brachii (straightens arm)

biceps brachii (bends elbow)

carpi radialis longus (helps move the wrist in many directions; it's the one you can feel bulge when you make a fist)

brachioradialis (rotates forearm and helps bend elbow)

The muscles in your arm are covered with connective tissue, too. That's what holds them together and gives them shape.

A muscle may look like a single unit, but it's made up of bundles of muscle fibers. Each fiber is a single muscle cell. The stapedius, the smallest muscle in the body, has about 1,500 muscle fibers. The biceps muscle in your arm has more than two million muscle fibers. And some of those muscle fibers—muscle cells—can be as long as 12 inches (30.48 centimeters).

Structure of Skeletal Muscle

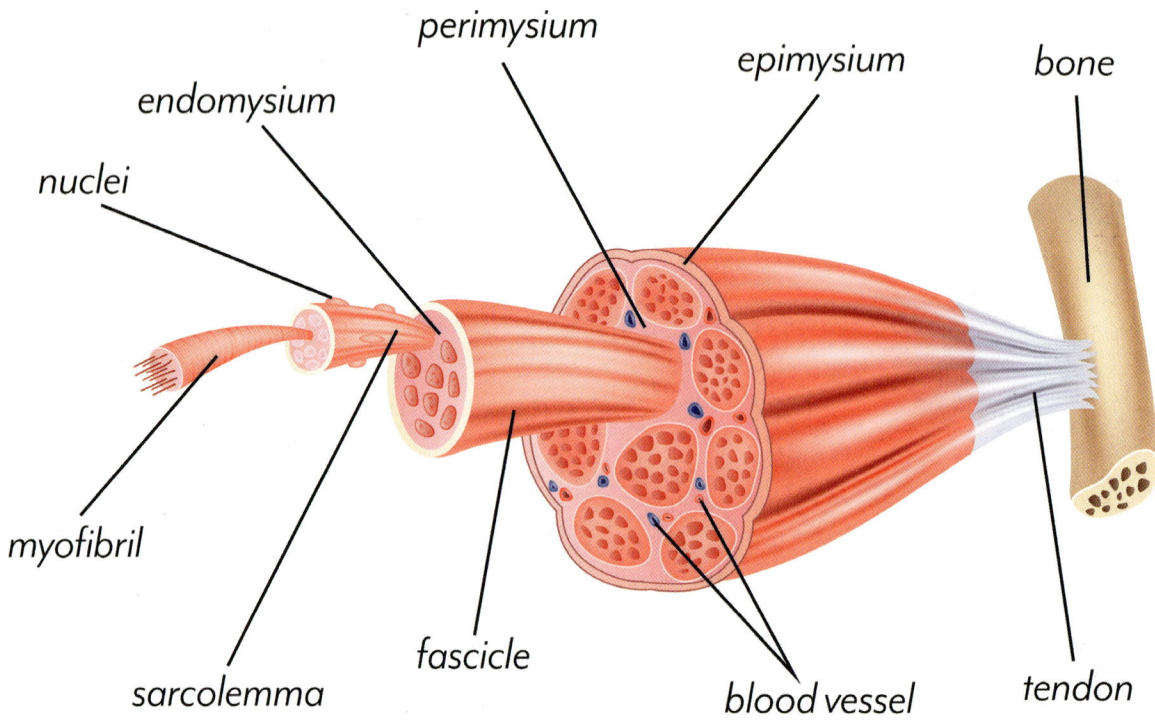

Each muscle fiber is made up of thread-like **myofibrils**. Inside each myofibril are hundreds of thick and thin **filaments**. Thick filaments are made of a protein called myosin. Thin filaments are made of another protein called actin. The way they overlap creates alternating light and dark bands, or striations.

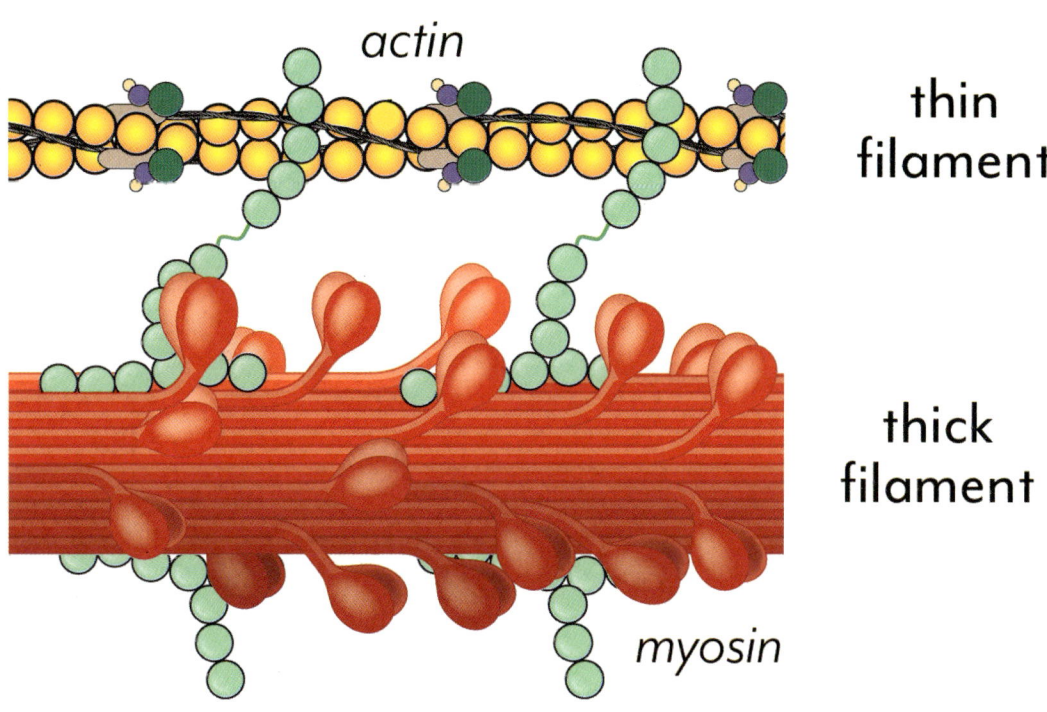

When you want to throw a ball, your brain sends a nerve signal to the muscles in your arm. That nerve impulse triggers the myosin filaments to pull on the actin filaments. The thick head of the myosin filament grabs onto the actin and pulls. It's like the way you would pull hand-over-hand on a rope in a tug of war.

As the myosin and actin filaments slide by each other, they make the muscle fibers shorten. The contraction of your upper arm muscle makes your arm bend as you get ready to throw.

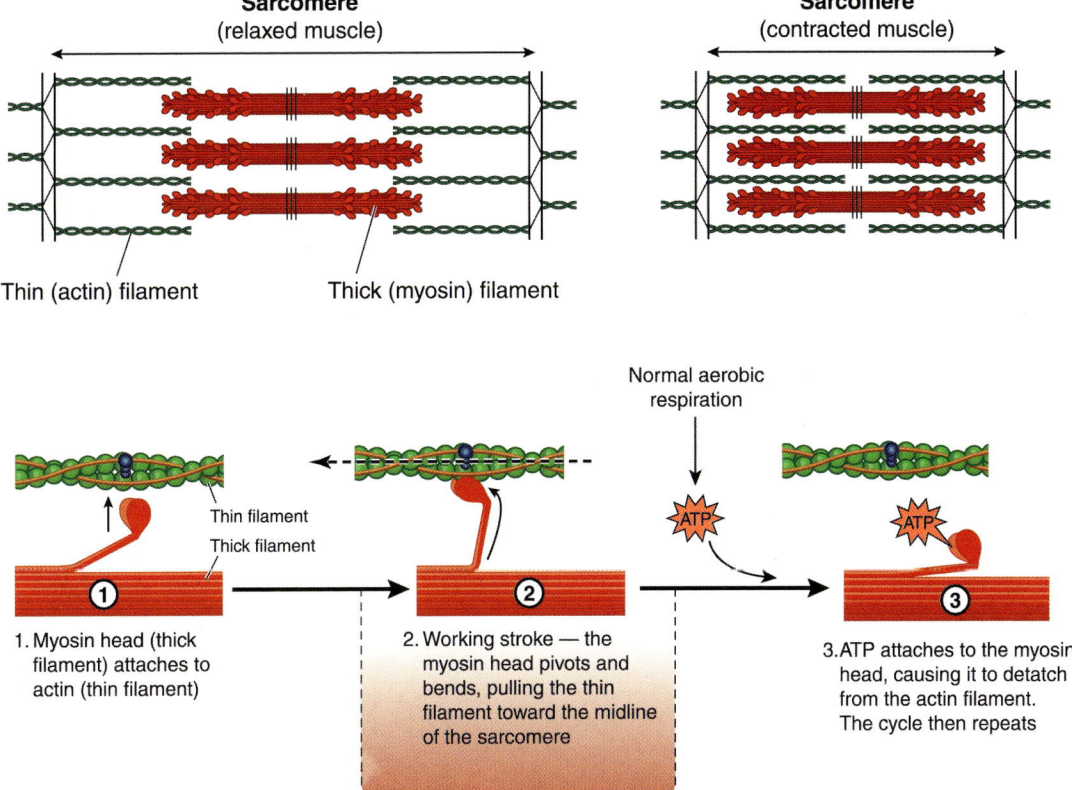

Calcium is important for bones and teeth. It's important for muscles too! Calcium is needed to trigger muscle contractions. Without calcium, the myosin head can't grab onto the actin filament. Not having enough calcium can cause muscle cramps in your legs.

MUSCLES MOVE US

Muscles can only pull (contract), not push, so they work in pairs. The biceps and triceps in your upper arm work together. The biceps muscle attaches to one of the bones in the forearm. When the biceps contracts it pulls on your lower arm to bend your elbow. The triceps muscle attaches to the other bone in the forearm. As the triceps contracts, it straightens the elbow. While the triceps is contracting, the biceps muscle relaxes.

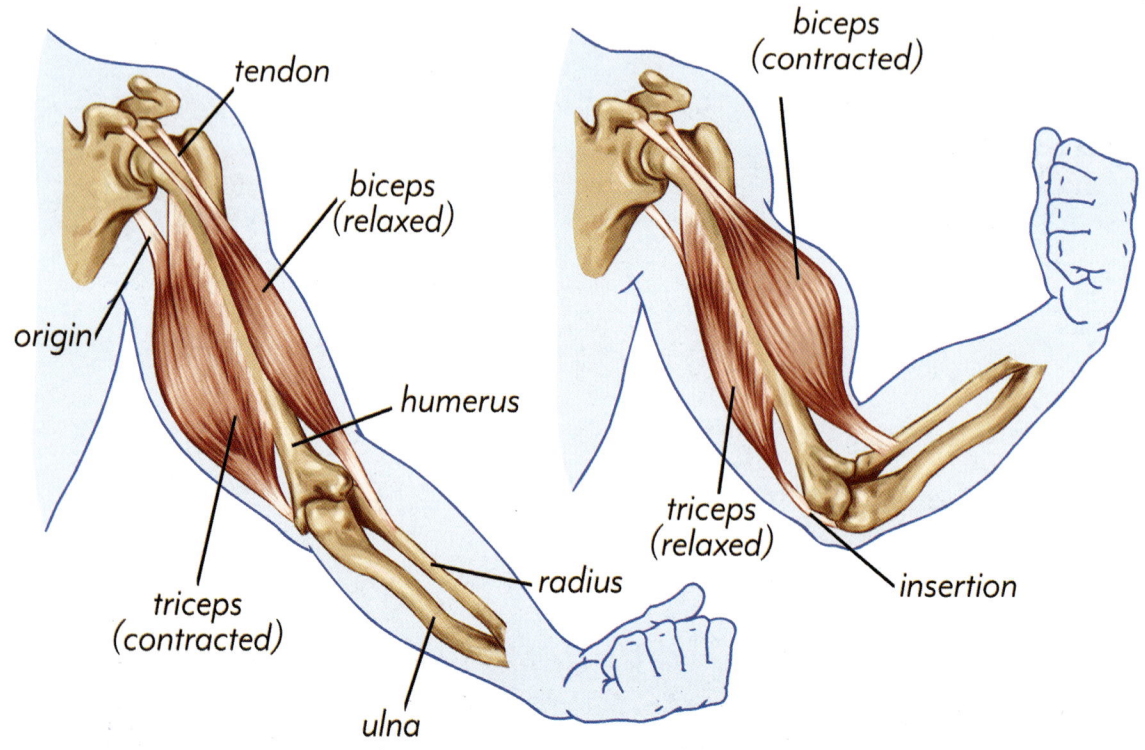

Same thing for your legs. The hamstring muscles in the back of your thigh contract to bend your knee. The quadriceps muscles in the front of the thigh contract to straighten your leg. Working together they get you walking, running, and climbing stairs. That's teamwork!

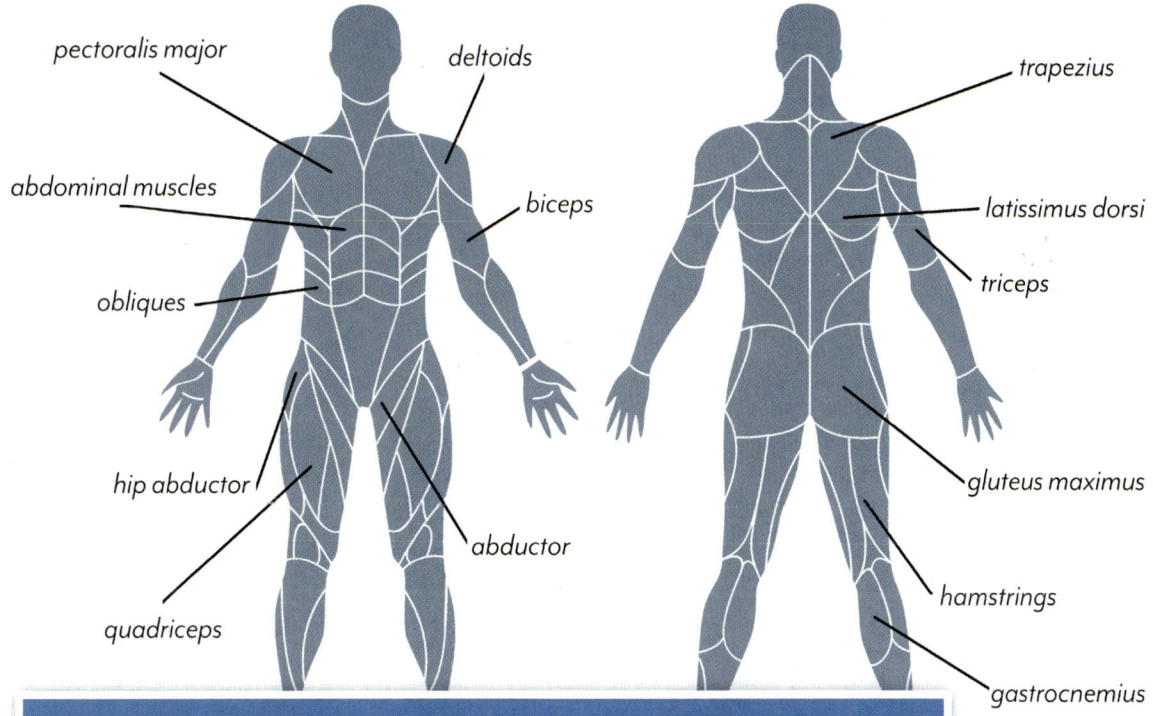

More Muscles to Know
Deltoid muscles move your shoulder to throw a ball or shrug.
Pectoralis muscles in your chest help you throw and lift.
Abdominal muscles help you breathe and keep you upright.
The *gluteus maximus muscle* is for more than sitting. It helps you walk and run.

Every time you look up, your neck muscles have to lift your heavy head. To make the job easier, they work with the bones at the top of your spine to create a **lever**. The simplest lever is a bar that lies across a pivot, just like a teeter totter. Push down on one end and the other end goes up. When you contract the muscles at the back of your neck, they pull down on one end of the lever. The other end tilts your chin up.

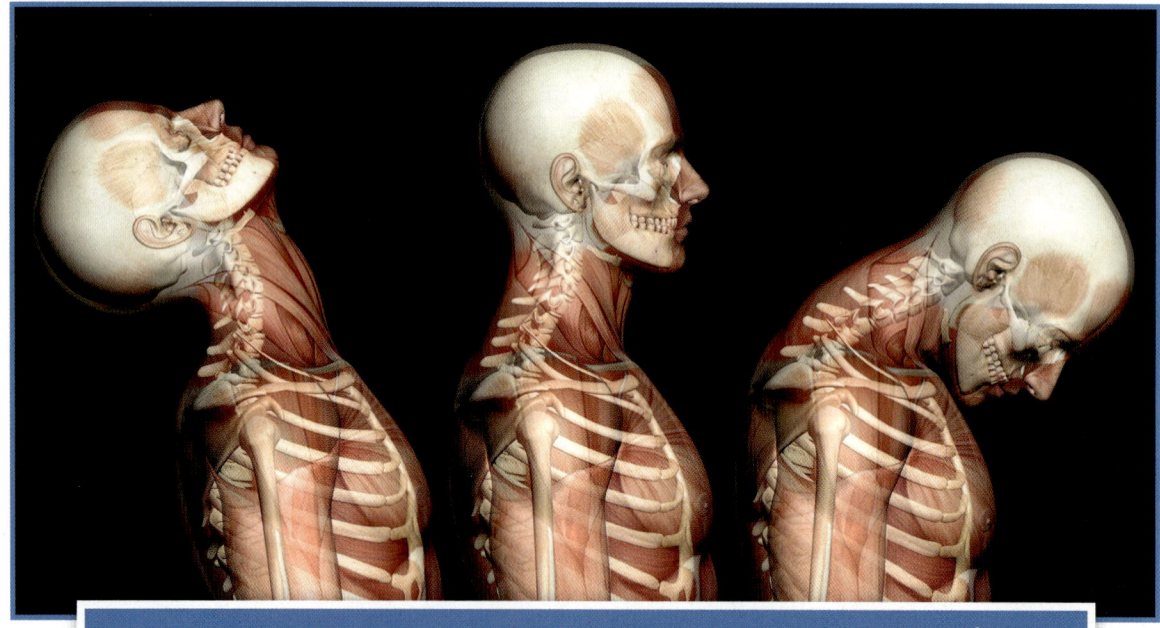

The head of an average adult weighs 10 pounds (4.5 kilograms). To get an idea of how much that is, put two five-pound (2.3 kilogram) bags of sugar in a bag. Now pick it up with one hand and lift it. Heavy, right?

When you stand on your toes your foot acts as a lever. That's a second-class lever, similar to how a wheelbarrow works. Bending your elbow uses a third-class lever. That's because the biceps muscle attaches to the bone between the joint (pivot) and the hand. This arrangement allows small contractions in the biceps to produce big movements in the arm.

Muscle Levers

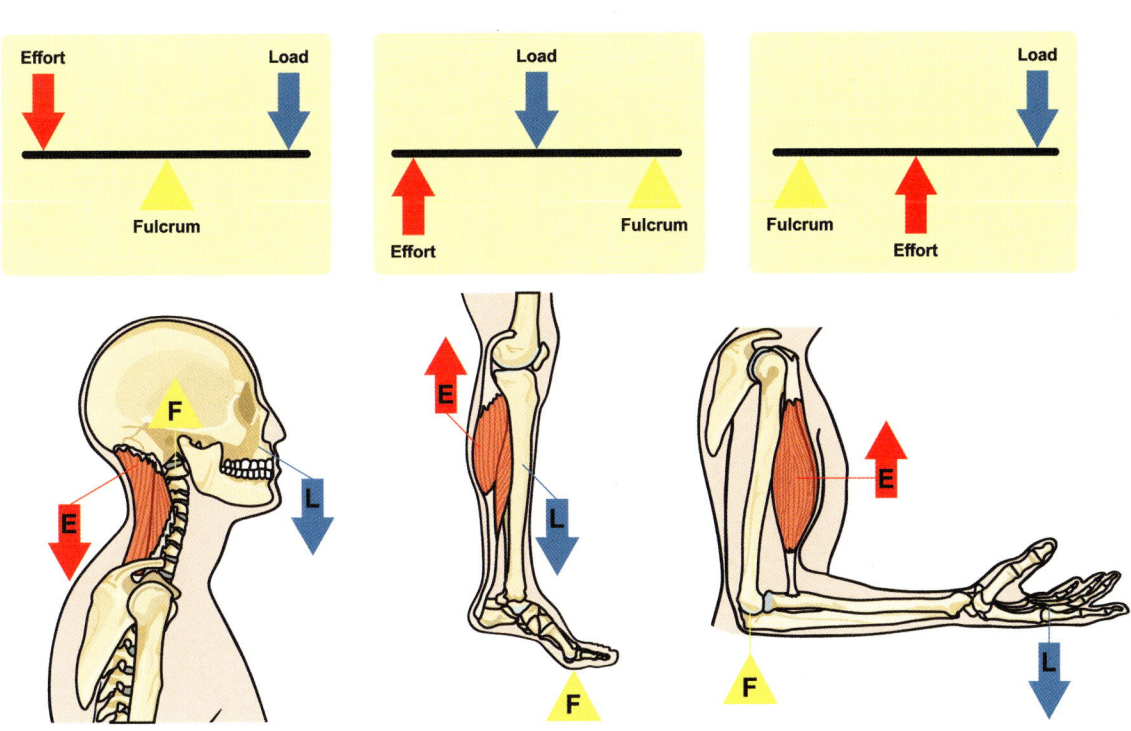

Taking Care of Your Muscles

Muscles need energy to do their jobs. They get their energy from carbohydrates—cereal, fruits, whole wheat crackers. To function properly, they need minerals such as iron, potassium, and calcium. Spinach, bananas, sweet potatoes, and dairy products are good sources of muscle minerals.

banana

spinach

sweet potatoes

Muscles need protein to repair themselves. Good protein sources are cheese, almonds, yogurt, or tuna on crackers. Muscles also need water to stay healthy. Water carries calcium and other **nutrients** into the muscle cells.

tuna

almonds

dairy

Make sure your muscles get lots of physical activity. They need at least an hour a day to stay healthy. When you don't use your muscles, they grow weak. The more you play, the stronger your muscles get. Physical activity keeps your heart muscle strong too. Not only that, activity can make you feel happier!

Great activities that help keep your muscles strong:

baseball	martial arts
basketball	row or paddle a boat
bike riding	soccer
cartwheels	skating
climb ropes	swimming
dancing	play on monkey bars
flying kites	tag
frisbee	tennis
hockey	tug-of-war
hopscotch	volleyball
hula-hoops	wheelbarrow races
jump rope	yoga
kickball	

SPRAINS AND STRAINS

Sometimes muscles get injured. A strain is a torn or pulled muscle or tendon. This can happen if you change direction quickly while running. Or if you lift too much weight.

A sprain happens when a **ligament** gets stretched or torn. Ligaments are bands of tissue that connect one bone to another. So sprains happen to joints, such as the elbow, knee, and ankle. The most common cause is falling or twisting.

Ankle Sprains

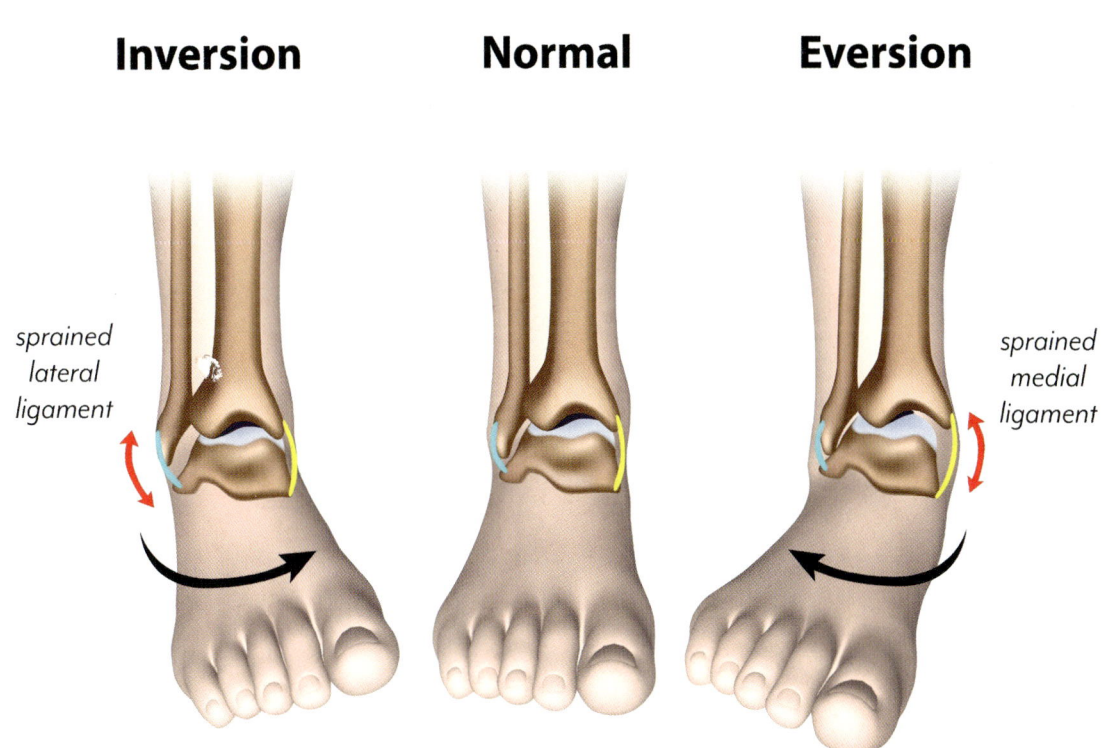

Inversion — sprained lateral ligament

Normal

Eversion — sprained medial ligament

27

Spending too much time on smartphones and tablets can result in a muscle problem called "text neck." The pain in the neck, upper back, shoulder, and arms is only part of the problem. When you're hunched over, the lungs can't expand fully.

That means you don't get as much oxygen as you should. So your heart has to pump harder to move blood faster to make up for the decreased oxygen level.

So sit up straight. Bring the smartphone or tablet up to eye level to read messages. Better yet—put down the phone and go play.

CHECK YOUR BODY POSTURE

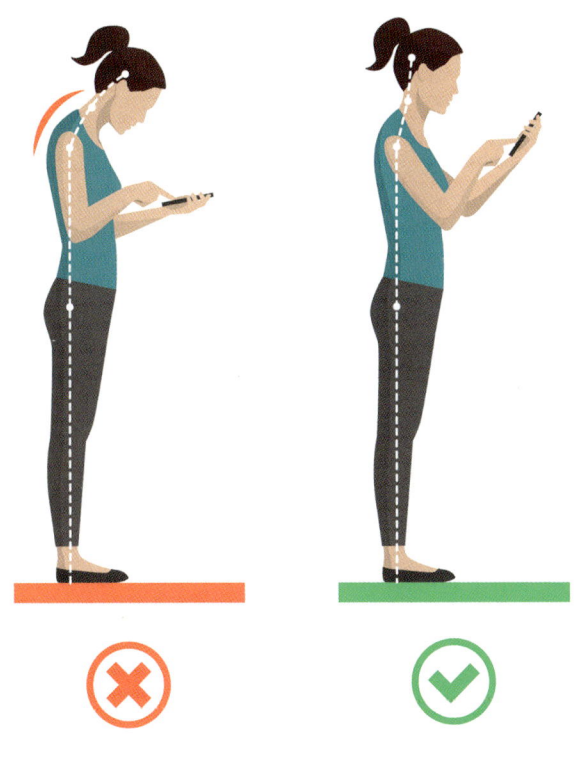

GLOSSARY

contracts (kuhn-TRACTS): makes something smaller

filaments (FIL-uh-muhnts): delicate and thin, threadlike structures

involuntary (in-VOL-uhn-ter-ee): done on its own, without you making it happen

lever (LEV-ur): a bar used to lift or move something

ligament (LIG-uh-muhnt): a band of tissue that connects one bone to another

myofibrils (mye-oh-FYE-bruhls): long, thin fibers that run parallel to each other and make up a muscle fiber

nutrients (NOO-tree-uhnts): substances needed for healthy growth and development

striated (STRI-ay-tuhd): marked with bands or wide stripes

tissue (TISH-yoo): a layer or mass of cells of the same kind that perform a certain job in the body

voluntary (VOL-uhn-ter-ee): done on purpose

INDEX

actin 15, 16, 17
cardiac muscles 5, 7, 10, 11
contraction(s) 17, 18, 19, 21
fiber(s) 11, 14, 15, 17
lever(s) 20, 21
myosin 15, 16, 17
pairs 18
protein 15, 23
skeletal muscles 5, 6, 7, 8, 10, 12
smooth muscle(s) 5, 7, 9
sprain 26, 27
strain 26
tendon(s) 8, 26

SHOW WHAT YOU KNOW

1. What are the three kinds of muscle tissue and where do you find them?
2. What is the difference between voluntary and involuntary muscles?
3. Name some muscles you use every day.
4. Why do skeletal muscles work in pairs?
5. What activities do you do to keep your muscles strong?

FURTHER READING

Canavan, Thomas, *How Many Muscles Make Your Smile? Questions About Muscles and Movement,* Power Kids, 2017.

Daniels, Patricia, Wilsdon, Christina and Agresta, Jen, *Ultimate Bodypedia: An Amazing Inside-Out Tour of the Human Body,* National Geographic Children's Books, 2014.

Farndon, John, *Stickmen's Guide to Your Mighty Muscles and Bones,* Hungry Tomato, 2017.

About the Author

Sue Heavenrich writes magazine articles and books for children. She taught science, wrote for newspapers, and develops programs for the local library. She lives in upstate New York where she uses her muscles to ski across the hay fields, plant tomatoes, and do tai chi.

Meet The Author!
www.meetREMauthors.com

© 2019 Rourke Educational Media

All rights reserved. No part of this book may be reproduced or utilized in any form or by any means, electronic or mechanical including photocopying, recording, or by any information storage and retrieval system without permission in writing from the publisher.

www.rourkeeducationalmedia.com

PHOTO CREDITS: Cover & Title Pg ©Orla, Pg 3 ©By adike, Pg 4 ©Steve Debenport, Pg 5 ©By DM7, Pg 6 ©By Sedova Elena, Pg 7 ©By BlueRingMedia, Pg 8 ©By BlueRingMedia, Pg 9 ©wiki, Pg 10 ©Hank Grebe, Pg 11 ©SPL, Pg 12 ©By jerrysa, Pg 13 ©By Ramona Kaulitzki, Pg 14 ©By Teguh Mujiono, Pg 15 ©By Blamb, Pg 16 ©RichVintage, Pg 17 ©By Blamb, Pg 18 ©By stihii, Pg 19 ©By Lina_Lisichka, Pg 20 ©angelhell, Pg 21 ©By udaix, Pg 22 ©Diy13, ©vasiliki, ©mariusFM77, Pg 23 ©Thomas Francois, ©fcafotodigital, ©kaanates, Pg 24 ©Wavebreakmedia, Pg 25 ©skodonnell, Pg 26 ©By Maridav, Pg 27 ©By Alila Medical Media, Pg 28 ©Jcomp, Pg 29 ©elenab

Edited by: Keli Sipperley
Cover design by: Rhea Magaro-Wallace
Interior design by: Kathy Walsh

Library of Congress PCN Data

How Muscles Work / Sue Heavenrich
(The Human Machine)
ISBN 978-1-64156-435-9 (hard cover)
ISBN 978-1-64156-561-5 (soft cover)
ISBN 978-1-64156-681-0 (e-Book)
Library of Congress Control Number: 2018930464

Rourke Educational Media
Printed in the United States of America,
North Mankato, Minnesota